The Idea Robot

by Meish Goldish

illustrated by Jeremy Tugeau

Harcourt

SCHOOL PUBLISHERS

Printed in the United States of America

ISBN 10: 0-15-350595-8
ISBN 13: 978-0-15-350595-9

Ordering Options
ISBN 10: 0-15-350336-X (Grade 6 Below-Level Collection)
ISBN 13: 978-0-15-350336-8 (Grade 6 Below-Level Collection)
ISBN 10: 0-15-357740-1 (package of 5)
ISBN 13: 978-0-15-357740-6 (package of 5)

2 3 4 5 6 7 8 9 10   179   12 11 10 09 08 07

Brian couldn't have been happier. He received a new robot for his birthday. Aunt Pam and Uncle Sid gave it to him. They said the robot was special.

"How is it different from all my other robots?" Brian asked.

"This one won't just do work for you," Uncle Sid explained. "It will think for you, too. You'll never need to think for yourself again."

"How is that possible?" Brian asked.

Aunt Pam smiled. "We fed the robot lots of information about you," she said. "It knows your favorite colors and your favorite books and games."

"In addition to those things, it knows your favorite foods," Uncle Sid added.

Brian contemplated his new gift. He smiled widely. "Thank you, Aunt Pam and Uncle Sid!" he cried. "I like my gift. Now I just need to give it a name. No, wait! I'll let the robot think of one for me."

Brian turned to the robot. "Robot, what should I call you?" he asked.

The robot's lights flashed. "TIR is a good name," the robot said. "It stands for *The Idea Robot*. I am TIR, the robot. I will give you good ideas."

"That's amazing!" Brian cried. "TIR really thinks for me!"

That afternoon, Brian sat contentedly at home. Then he phoned his friend, Gail. "Come over," he told her. "I want to show you something."

Gail soon arrived. "Meet TIR," Brian said to her. "He's my new robot. Watch what he can do."

Brian turned to TIR. "TIR, I'm thirsty," he said. "What should I drink?"

TIR's lights flashed. "Drink a glass of orange juice," the robot replied. "Drink a glass of orange juice."

Gail's eyes grew wide. "Wow!" she cried. "I've seen a lot of boring robots, but I'd have no qualms about owning this one!"

Brian said, "This Saturday is Tina's birthday party. I wonder what shirt I should wear." Brian turned to his new robot. "TIR, what should I wear to Tina's birthday party?"

TIR's lights flashed and blinked. "Wear your bright blue shirt. Wear your bright blue shirt," TIR said.

"I love that shirt!" Brian cried. "Blue is my favorite color. TIR, you sure know how to think! Thank you!"

All day, Brian asked TIR a torrent of questions. TIR answered each one. He gave Brian one idea after another. Brian and Gail were amazed.

Brian said, "TIR, I want to play a game. What should I play?"

TIR's lights blinked. "Play a game of checkers. Play a game of checkers," TIR said. "I will play against you."

"Wow!" Gail cried. "TIR can play games, too. Will he tell you how to beat him?"

"Let's find out," Brian replied. He began to set up the checkers on the board. Then he decided to let TIR do it instead.

TIR mechanically placed the checkers on the board, one at a time. He did it without error. When he finished, he beeped to let Brian know he was ready to play.

"Which color should I be?" Brian asked.

"You be red. I'll be black," TIR replied.

TIR and Brian started to play. "You move first," TIR said. The robot pointed to one of Brian's checkers. "Move this one to here," TIR said in an officious voice. Brian did as he was told.

The game continued. TIR told Brian every move to make. The robot made its own moves, too. Soon TIR was winning.

"See if TIR will let you win," Gail said.

Brian looked at the robot. "TIR, what should I do to win the game?" he asked.

TIR pointed to one of Brian's checkers. "Move this one to here. Then I'll move that one to there. Then you jump me three times. Then you win the game."

Brian and Gail both laughed. Gail said, "Surely if TIR knows what you will do, he will make a different move. He won't want to lose, right?"

"I don't know," Brian said.

Brian did what TIR said. Sure enough, he won the checkers game.

"That was easy," Gail said.

"Yes," Brian agreed, "but it wasn't much fun. TIR was supposed to play against me. However, he wasn't contrary at all. In fact, he helped me. I won without even thinking."

"Brian, you can win every time without trying at all!" Gail said.

"I know," Brian sighed. "That's the problem."

Brian got up from the table. "Let's do something else, Gail," he said.

TIR's lights flashed and blinked. "Read a mystery story," the robot said. "Read a mystery story."

Brian frowned at TIR. "I didn't ask you for an idea," he said. "I feel like going outside anyway."

"Ride your bike in the park," TIR said. "Ride your bike in the park."

"I'm finding this intolerable," Brian said.

Brian looked around the room. He saw a large towel. He placed it over the robot's head. "Maybe this will keep TIR quiet," he said.

Suddenly, TIR began to make funny noises. He squeaked and clanked. He honked and clattered. Brian and Gail looked at each other.

"Something's wrong," Brian said.

"You don't think TIR would endanger us, do you?" Gail asked.

Just then, TIR said, "Drink a bright blue shirt. Wear a glass of orange juice. Read a bike. Ride your book. I am TIR, the mystery checker in the park. The park, the park, the park . . ."

"TIR's out of control!" Brian cried. "How do we turn him off?"

"I have an idea," Gail said. "Pull the battery from his back." Brian did. The robot grew quiet.

"I guess I learned a good lesson," Brian laughed. "Sometimes it's better to think for yourself!"

Think Critically

1. How is TIR different from Brian's other robots?

2. Why is Brian sad about winning the checker game?

3. What does Brian learn about himself by the end of the story?

4. Do you think Brian will keep TIR? Why or why not?

5. Would you like a robot that does all your thinking for you? Explain.

 Science

Design a Robot Design a robot that does one or more special jobs. Explain in writing how the robot works. Draw a diagram to go with your explanation.

School-Home Connection Tell your family about the story. Then discuss some things you would like to have a robot do around your home and some things that are better left for humans to do.

Word Count: 945